Just What the Poet Ordered...

365 SHORT FORM POEMS FOR ALL OCCASIONS

BOBBIE ISABEL

The primary aim of poetry is to express and evoke emotion. Though these are short poems, there are some difficult and painful topics peppered throughout, including childhood trauma, trauma responses, mental illness, aging, loss, and relationship struggles. Please take care with your mental health, check the index for the location of the strongest poems of these topics, and read as you can, if you can.

Copyright © 2025
All rights reserved.
Paperback ISBN-13: 978-1-961045-28-6
Ebook ISBN-13: 978-1-961045-29-3

A Note from the Poet

For the past two years, I have released a topical collection of poetry during National Poetry Month. I had planned to skip this year, but my heart had other plans. For those who don't know me, poetry is how I got started writing. It was cathartic for me to get my emotions out on paper, and they all began flowing through verse.

From late 2021 through October 2024, I wrote over 600 poems, most of them haiku or other short forms. While many made it into my first two collections, so many more have been sitting in files. This collection came from me sifting through the files and realizing that I had written enough short-form poems for you to enjoy one a day for an entire year and not run out.

Thus, I present to you exactly what the poet ordered, a series of poems that can be enjoyed in many different ways. So, find what works for you. Binge them all if you want. Enjoy one a day. Check out the index for some topics, if there's something that ails you right now. Or simply open to a random page and enjoy.

January

1-1
Expressed through the eyes
Moved to tears
Built on fear
Obscured over time
Disguised as love
Youth stolen

1-2
Love sacrifices all when
We lack empathy.
Compassionate abscondence
Relies on courage
Surrendering nothing so
That integrity
perseveres in dark times...strong.

1-3

Nervous words

T
  u
   m
   b
   l
    e

From my fingers

Onto the page

———

1-4

memories jarred from

long-forgotten hiding space

glisten with fresh tears

———

1-5

bending my body

ensnaring all my senses

crashing sweet release

———

1-6

Just like clockwork

She stands poised

Her demons' arrive

1-7

Walk through the playground—

images of childhood missed

a peace never known

1-8

how much is too much—

bodies more regulated

than weapons of death

1-9

less like a flipped switch

more like a dimmer frozen—

emotions don't work

1-10

peaceful wishes are

the feel of soft vibrations—

kitten contentment

———

1-11

speak easy living

gin and vermouth, bourbon twist

inhibition melts

———

1-12

Shadows of our forgotten

relationship

Bathed

In

Blue

Light

———

1-13

knightly eyes ablaze

damsel off slaying demons

removing armor

———

1-14

grown intelligence

she felt the weight of the world

on her young shoulders

———

1-15

accusations fly

friendships stand in the balance

they wait for respite

———

1-16

shadow figures dance

haze hides the waxing outline

waves lap at the sand

———

1-17

the tree shouldn't bow

before the majestic snow—

the weight on its bough

———

1-18

see age as blessing

time is uncontrollable

though we keep trying

———

1-19

In times of great tumult

Solitude brings peaceful clarity

———

1-20

Through the trauma

And unending fear

We press on

———

1-21

Truth

Words

Flowing

Taking shape

Spilling on paper

Creative release of pressure

1-22

plight invisible

stuck suffering in silence

wanting to be whole

1-23

slipping through fingers

dark images careening

avoiding the page

brittle edges of my mind

frayed from forgotten battles

1-24

Daydreams

and

Nightmares:

Two halves

of the

Same

Coin

1-25

fighting the changes

logical thought out windows

hormonal crisis

1-26

magical tendrils

swimming through gossamer skies

ocean life in flight

1-27

Heartfelt apologies

Earnest consideration

Achieved presence of mind

Loving the process

Internalized appreciation

Negativity at a minimum

Growing aspirations

1-28

Poetry is healing when the pain is too much.

Poetry is peace when the world is chaotic.

Poetry is love when the emptiness invades.

Poetry is hope that our words will outlive us.

Poetry is trust that the clouds will part.

Poetry is faith that we will persevere.

1-29

scent soothes:

Rain on dirt

and

Snow in air

1-30

Most likely to lose

Rights

Highly likely to feel

Taken

Very likely to struggle

Alone

More likely to die

Pregnant

1-31

Food bowl is empty

All doors are closed

Litter needs cleaning

Water dripped on my nose

Got them cat-astrophe blues.

February

2-1
Putty in his hands
Chocolate on his lips
Pliable

2-2
bruised egos and scars—
reminders of aimlessly
wandering through life

2-3
Laying,
Head in
Your lap,
Heart in
Your hands

2-4

A heady combination

Your strength

Against my softer side

2-5

hands slowly slide up

as arms encircle my waist

pulse quickening fast

2-6

just like most fruit, some

words have more bite than others—

forbidden still life

2-7

the sky bedazzled

shades of black, blue and purple:

galaxies aligned

2-8

Our fingers

Intertwined

Like vines

Holding

Against all

Crosswinds

2-9

the ice in my soul

craves the fire in your heartbeat

complementing needs

2-10

nothing stings more than

the scolding you didn't get—

life lessons are hard

2-11

walk through abandoned

remnants of patients long gone

mental health matters

———

2-12

Without you

House echoes empty

Notes fall flat

Alone

———

2-13

Your fingers

On my skin

Pluck pizzicato

Heartbeat tuned

———

2-14

luxurious buy—

plucking eloquent beauty

opened buds short lived

2-15

Never cartwheeled

But I

Tripped

And

Fell

For you

2-16

As sure as

The mountains peak

I am yours

2-17

I've lost my marbles

Hungry, hungry, who's to say

How the hippos play

2-18

infinity lasts

daybreak is night's long goodbye

lonely hearts lament

2-19

glimpses of time lost

staggering between teardrops

memories unfold

2-20

Captivated, tongue

tied, enthralled

with words—

the poetry of

YOU

2-21

Innate talent

Shelved passion

Creativity sparked from pages of words

Characters brought to life in images

Inspiration growing

Promises kept

2-22

Lying in bed

Dreaming a picturesque window

Waves lapping the shore

Cuddled in your arms

Waiting for the sun to shine

2-23

Articulated daydream

Cut off by the shining moon

Night crestfallen

Shrouds of darkness

Bathing festered scars

Nectar of sweet nothing

Longing for sunlight

Awash in perpetual anticipation

2-24

Us

Soft

Playful

Comfortable

A pair of

Unmatched

Socks

2-25

memories trigger

misty mornings in sunlight—

dewdrops turn teardrops

2-26

Arguments aside

Love is the hill

I'll live

Upon

2-27

In laughter

In tears

I turn to you

Breathless

2-28

Belittling

Empathy

Leads to

Inevitable heartache

Eloquent liars

Voicing

Excuses

March

3-1
risky management—
giving yourself permission
to feel smooth sailing

3-2
Gray days
Reflected in gray eyes
The perfect disguise

3-3
Settled...
Like a bill
A relationship
In, on
Broken

3-4

Eyes blurry from sleep

or binge scrolling endless feeds

she watches hours pass

3-5

what happened last night

reminders of poor choices

still lay strewn about

3-6

Uncertainty is...

self-deprecating jokes told

hidden behind laughs

3-7

the sound of raindrops

distraction from loneliness

remembered footsteps

3-8

Mornings bring clarity

Sun still shines

We still love

3-9

the face you put on

changes with time regardless—

acid tears melt masks

3-10

the calm soon broken

squalls of energy burst forth

tiny tornado

3-11

Storm approaching

Graying sky

Wind chimes warning

Tinkling bells

3-12

spring rains flower buds

memories of grandma's house

the smell of mildew

3-13

cottage in the wood

ivy overtaken walls

showing aged disuse

3-14

social media

influence and red carpet

the lights fade from view

3-15

gearing up for spring

daffodils already bloomed

second winter comes

3-16

forever smiling

ev'rything is a wonder

wide-eyed toddler girl

3-17

Uncomfortable

Surrounded

Overwhelmed

Quiet

Watchful

Exhausted

Slipping Out

Escape

3-18

Her very presence

Amidst trivia and crime

His being does crave.

3-19

cemetery's hush

during our evening walk

we move in silence

3-20

wind blows 'neath dark clouds

seasonal changes coming

seedlings sprout first cut

3-21

floral scents bursting

new life fluttering spring breeze

powdery green cars

3-22

fear irrational

spectacular weekend trip

until the ground shook

3-23

out of desolation

bright yellow bursts faithfully

reminders of spring

3-24

early arrivals

reminder that spring returns

surprised by march frost

3-25

joy, pain and sorrow

felt year-round, yet in springtime

tears hide in downpours

3-26

seasonal rain taunts

promises of fine flowers

brings migraines and weeds

3-27

Windy days

Spread

Spring seeds

And

Autumn leaves

Around

3-28

moisture marinade—

fertilizing flatlands for

mushroom multitudes

3-29

pitter patter rain

ripples of waves in puddles

power of nature

3-30

love is a basket

full of brightly colored smiles—

sometimes clouds rain down

3-31

delicate scented

springtime daydreams pink and white

cherry blossom blooms

April

4-1
Excuses justify
actions
inexcusable
Justice holds
inexcusable actions
accountable

4-2
after shower earth
sweet smell of azalea blooms
color fandango

4-3

Empty stems

Blooms strewn

Thorns withered

Plucked too soon

———

4-4

weeks of steady rain

saturated seedlings grow

garden begs for mow

———

4-5

grass is cut neatly

bushes trimmed in perfect form

sinuses scream "help!"

———

4-6

Walking through a field of dreams

hand in hand in Spring

Chill in the air

Sun in the sky

Crystalline dreams at our feet

propelling us forward

toward the future

holding fast to the present

4-7

deep in the forest

at the depth of the river

lay a sword of myth

4-8

shout out to all the

late bloomers in lilac hues...

your colors still shine

4-9

numbness plagues like scars

both problem and cure for pain—

the goal is to feel

———

4-10

terrace smells alive

fresh dirt and new flower blooms—

enchantments of spring

———

4-11

fan out your feathers

little bird, as you let go—

bravely leave the nest

———

4-12

spring showers drown

winter doldrums with flowers

news at eleven

———

4-13

young cubs play and fight

learning to fend for themselves

the circle of life

4-14

forgotten childhood

memories of woodland walks

holes left in the heart

4-15

Sluggish

Wanderings

Trudging

Muddy shoes

Pristine carpets

Stained

Memories

Imprinted

4-16

flowers pollinate

spreading beauty east to west

give thanks for the bees

4-17

blooms scent stagnant air

breezes enter long-closed doors

hallmarks of springtime

4-18

rana toma sol

rodeado por loto—

cuento de ada

frog sunbathes safe

surrounded by lotus leaves—

what a fairytale

4-19

caterpillar thoughts

upon nestling in cocoons:

we must all fly free

but first we must melt away

dissolving from existence

———

4-20

radiant release

resting buds reawaken

to a bee's delight

———

4-21

winter turns to spring

daylight lengthens as warmth spreads

darks dawns to flowers

———

4-22

listen to the trees

crackling torments whispered screams

the planet has much to say

4-23

sign of spring renewal—

apple blossoms in the trees

rain smells in the air

4-24

triumphant battle—

snow melted, coat stored, sunshine

spoils of the long war

welcoming seasons of change

remove the mask of winter

4-25

sunny april morn

perfect blossoms triumphant—

summer is coming

4-26

Cloudy dreams

beset with storms

Turmoil within

fighting

shadows

4-27

Sing little blackbird

Feared or revered

Raven or crow

4-28

Clouds signaling storm

Trees dance a tambourine song

We drive for breakfast

4-29

rain pools in driveways

tinged with flecks of pollen green

spring's cool winds blow through

4-30

cabin fever ache

like butterfly cocoon sleep—

summer's sun calls me

May

5-1
eternal sadness—
an unbending mind coupling
an unyielding heart

5-2
Bliss is
Wearing
Your shirt
Basking
In your scent

5-3

Head resting

Listening to your heartbeat

Moment of peace

———

5-4

willful compliance—

bold blooms follow the sun in

any direction

———

5-5

like the fusion of

atoms crashing together

we have chemistry

———

5-6

Head on the grass

Eyes to the sky

Daydreaming

———

5-7

the quiet morning

birds chirping and cats sleeping

house silent at rest

5-8

distant aroma

honeysuckle and lilac

running through spring fields

5-9

the fountain of youth

holds no water for my life—

fall wrinkles smile yet

5-10

when he kissed her lips

she sprang alive in hushed tones—

the heat in her cheeks

5-11

humble beginnings

life of ups and downs follow

survival is key

5-12

two creative minds

aligned in complement paths

once in a lifetime

5-13

guess and check movements

relationships take us through

just like learning math

5-14

to put children first

and forget about yourself

fails the family

5-15

seed healing waters

of experience feeding

the garden of my soul

5-16

cyclical matter

butterflies erupt wings forth

As earth's view changes

5-17

Her story universal

Her body worn

Like leather-bound tomes

5-18

Each new chapter

Is a reminder

Editing is

Always

Possible

5-19

The birds

were singing,

quite pleased

to wake

the sun.

5-20

To emerge

From a nightmare

Untainted

Is no small feat.

5-21

head in the clouds like

augmented reality—

defied gravity

5-22

looking at floor plans

planning a future in style

how far we have come

5-23

birds silently wake

beneath a persimmon sky

calm before the storm

5-24

the way your mind thinks

unmarred youth experience

my broken soul sings

5-25

You are a classic example of a love poem unwritten.

5-26

Your absence

Sets my heart

Adrift looking

For anchor

5-27

Historical lies

Misplaced hate

Glaring inequities

Explosions of rage

5-28

short-lived blooms

beauty renewed yearly–

azalea in spring

5-29

cars lining the street

greasy streaks on the driveway

heartbreak on the wind

final chances for goodbyes

stolen by the forgetting

5-30

On the cliff

Poised for action

Tide coming in

5-31

house looking empty—

sweeping away cobwebs of

memories faded

June

6-1
Look of fear
at sunset
Turns in triumph
Sunrise

6-2
The past
And
The future
D
O
W
N
a gravel road

6-3

I hear sounds of morning

Written in your eyes

———

6-4

old habits creep in

when we lose our perspective

and forget our dreams

———

6-5

infused spirit

soaked in liquor

drowning in distillation

intoxicated

———

6-6

risking reminiscent thought

fear lost in your memories

———

6-7

a tour in photos

the botanical gardens

Inevitably

6-8

colors have meaning—

blue the color of sadness

and the peaceful sky

6-9

always add a dash

of garlic and paprika

cooking is an art

6-10

vines must climb to reach

the sky through the canopy—

hoping the trees stand tall

6-11

the mist shifts trailing

clouds over the obscured bridge

airy suspension

6-12

Stay the course.

Play the course.

Tiring?

Of course!

6-13

Shock

Tears

Anger

Collapse

Counseling

Rebuilding

From the

Rubble

6-14

the damage of could

awash in the memories

of painful regret

6-15

glistening droplets

sun peeking behind dark clouds

dusty rock rinsed clean

6-16

Set adrift

On waves

Of hope I

Shutter

Out

Pain

6-17

The earth was silent

Though the air spoke

Wind bringing messages

Through the atmosphere

Hermes wings

Hurtling wishes across plains

Like dandelion breaths

6-18

Dragonfly in mist

reflected on a blue sky

happiness dawning

6-19

Trust is but an illusion

A promise of afterlife

6-20

heartbeat of droplets

exotic sway of branches

summer rain movements

6-21

use it or lose it...

I spoke fluent toddlerese

twenty years ago

6-22

moss swaying on trees

shadowy impression of

wispy willow tears

6-23

drive

smooth tunes

vibes

6-24

smell of clean linen

dancing in the summer breeze

grandma's house memoirs

6-25

unplanned escape route—

impromptu scenic road trip

through back road detours

6-26

across steep chasms

feats of engineering stand

withstanding time

6-27

Doohickeys.

Thingamajigs.

Watchamacallits.

There is nothing like

The right tool for the job.

Explicitly fashioned to fit.

Purposeful in its nature.

Could I use a knife? Of course.

Any old pen will do, but why settle?

6-28

a tad, bit, or smidge

ways we describe big feelings

our own love language

6-29

morning professions—

loving words beautiful as

starlings murmuring

6-30

uninspired writing

stringing random words for prompts

very challenging

July

7-1
Sunlight darkened
Sound silenced
Water burned
Love numbed
Apocalypse

7-2
Standing
On a
Precipice
Life looks
Up at me

7-3

Accept the ante

Deal the cards

Hearts drawn

Fold

7-4

Foresee me

In smoldering ash

Nestled and warm

Dying

7-5

first rays of sunlight

my toes blanketed by sand

the world falls away

7-6

feet firmly planted

sinking in the mired wasteland

lonely is success

7-7

slow and steady slide

gigantic and powerful:

glaciers move mountains

7-8

Discovery Plus

capturing cats' hearts and minds

one shark at a time

7-9

I collect tears like

lakes catch rain after a drought—

jars of memories

7-10

news coverage leaking

uncertainty reigns anew

anxiety raised

7-11

Draw of card

Roll of dice

Life of chance

7-12

Twenty-nine years

Babies don't bounce

But time flies

7-13

Random fact—

My introvert heart

Loves

A Blackjack table

7-14

sounds of kids' laughter

and open fire hydrants

summer has arrived

7-15

strokes of summer heat—

molten lava streaks across

an azure landscape

7-16

Who might we have been

If trauma didn't get us first

If nightmares hadn't

Overshadowed dreams

If our bodies had been our own

And our minds had been free

Uncluttered for creativity?

7-17

Feel deeply

See clearly

Listen closely

Believe in

Your truth

7-18

We belong

In daydreams

Lucid and colorful

Like sunrise along the shore

Where everything

Glimmers free

And happy

7-19

Cracks in the ceiling

Settled with age

Like wrinkles and crows' feet

Setting the stage

For the telling of stories

From the most sage

For wisdom comes slowly

With turns of a page

7-20

Rooted in depths of blue water

Buoyant in your radiance

We float at your whim

Hovering protectively

Watching you reign

And giving you reins

Over our hearts

As you grow

Surrounded

By love

7-21

the struggle is real

the pieces don't fit inside

the frame that I built

leaving my mind to puzzle

the strength of my perception

7-22

yearling poetry

reminder of a weak voice

strengthened over time

7-23

rainy saturday

weekend travel plans ruined

consolation naps

7-24

bold summer blooms cast

perfect redolent netting—

lone bee enticement

7-25

i sing a cat's purr

sinewy smooth vibrations—

content in your arms

7-26

Few have smooth rides

Most are

```
    p              d
  m  y  d  j  e
  u     n    a g
  B     a    g
```

7-27

I miss your fingers

the way they played on my neck

smooth legato

———

7-28

anticipation

piqued at notifications

boxes at the door

———

7-29

trauma driven crack

filled with golden filigree

broken in her strength

———

7-30

they seem quiet now

yet mischief is their passion

they scream at closed doors

———

7-31

i never start fights

it's hard not to take the bait

when your heart's at stake.

August

8-1
Ambling through life
(Arthritis clicks,
Muscles ache)
with grace

8-2
You apologize
For rambling
I'm caught
On your
Lips

8-3

In a dry world

Love is a

Humid

Reprieve

8-4

something about you

calls to my innermost needs:

an orchestral voice

8-5

Thinking of you—

Your smiling eyes

Your perceptive touch

8-6

to look beautiful

smell appealing and feed bees

flowers have purpose

8-7

summer flowerings

keep bees returning for more—

nectar's siren song

8-8

a strong bass line takes

him on a natural high—

road trips are the best

8-9

memories pervade

consciousness like open apps

baring hidden files

8-10

veiny fingers reach

toward the dark sky in dry hope

preparing for rain

8-11

sauce, purée, peaches

in jars ready for winter

shelved in memory

8-12

never good enough

seeking praise that would not come

striving for her best

8-13

promises unkept

for expectations untold–

the sad end of love

8-14

beneath scorching temps

midsummer eyes turn to fall

flower petals drift

8-15

triumph as dawn peaks

the elusive prize was won

sleep and rest renewed

8-16

Escape

from

the

mundane

Daydreams

impossible

the

for

Prepare

8-17

perennial seed

geraniums bloom when

summer's sun shines bright

8-18

Still

Calm

Waters

Belie truth

Heavy turbulence

Hiding just beneath the surface

8-19

ever vigilant

xenomorphic intentions

cosplaying friendship

8-20

sorrowful landscape

history-filled ashes float

across xeric fields

8-21

belted high notes are

the wellspring of happiness

theatre is home

8-22

rite of passage cast

wayfare paid in white roses

dirt buried boxes

8-23

tunnel of shadow

imagination vista

fantasy ahead

8-24

arms raised fingers spread

vermillion petals waiting—

promises of rain

8-25

Us, comfortable, worn leather seats

Built in middle school

Before either of us could drive

Dented but everything still works

Miles between us, covered

By tuned-up phone calls

Every three to five months

———

8-26

organized chaos

due dates, projects, to do list

rescued by post-its

———

8-27

lost, tossed, and battered

seashells wait in shifting sands

for morning's sunrise

———

8-28

listen for the crowds

the hurried rush of wheeled carts

the beach strewn with trash

8-29

hiding in the brush

she heard the others screaming

and took off running

8-30

My soul

Cries

For your heat

Of endless

Summer

8-31

adrenaline rush

crossing the land bridge at dawn

high tide laughs at them.

September

9-1
September first
Harbinger of
Sweater weather
Comfy sweats
Shorter days

9-2
Turn on mute
Lighten the mood
Change the view

9-3

saying it's enough

yet pushing through achiness

follow own advice

9-4

preserved rose petals

paper printed with red ink

memories like thorns

9-5

the power of yet—

experience teaches us

possibilities

9-6

dulcet tones in verse

captivating melodies

your voice calls to me

9-7

wishes like whispers

written on a painted sky

dreaming in the midst

———

9-8

forget woes and let

dreams manifest happy thoughts—

where singing birds wake

———

9-9

leaves rattle upturned

trunks bow low as branches wave

storms rage in response

———

9-10

no need to ask for

permission or where you fit

vines make their own way

———

9-11

at birth aging starts

life begs the question of death

existential dread

9-12

mindsets play a part

in our interpretations—

of peace and chaos

9-13

words set to smooth music

dreams built for the theater

talents intertwined

9-14

fox watches daylight

awaiting cool mist of dusk

curled up in its den

9-15

rate of words written

in inverse proportion to

minutes spent scrolling

9-16

shrieks for aid unheard

who will answer the trees call

as vines grow tighter

9-17

dips in the sand mark

the ebb and flow of time as

ancient waves buckle

9-18

Postcards sent home

Memories traveling

Through space

and

Time stamped

9-19

lazy lake living

convertible driving days

end of summer comes

9-20

She awoke

With delight

At Fall's

Cool air

Touch

9-21

the beauty of fall

cooler temperatures mean

the end of fruit flies

9-22

possibility

endless collection of words

crossword puzzling

9-23

sounds of joyful days

baby laughs and kitten purrs—

spirits uplifted

9-24

Though the sky be gray,

the thunder clash,

the rivers swell,

and

the wind howl,

the storm seems tame

against

the tempest in her eyes.

9-25

soft shadows passing

across the barely lit room—

trees and wind dancing

9-26

words can't describe the

profundity of my joy—

love letter from mom

9-27

lazy saturday

on the couch, game show playing

words captured on page

9-28

Your voice sings to me

On a timpani of anticipation

Breathy whispers on my skin

Its timbre an embrace

Within which I forget the world

And fold myself in its melody

9-29

we move socially

the lone wolf perishes or

wreaks havoc for all

9-30

Your Silence Whispers

Into the recesses if my psyche

Screaming obscenities

Into the void of insecurities

October

10-1
the promise of joy—
his sinister intention
to win her over

arrogance his great folly
she reveled in his torment

10-2
On the wall by the stair
Shadows of memory
Finely framed
Haunting
Marking the passage of time
With each step
Reminders of ghosts and
Demons long gone
But never forgotten

10-3

The road to greatness

Is paved with tears

Collected

10-4

think about your needs

be careful your requests match

people can't read minds

10-5

a digital nod

an ode to a simpler time:

analog watch face

10-6

wearing bell on neck

excellent at hide and seek

can't be found for hours

10-7

flowers bloom alone

no explanation needed

seek not permission

10-8

being good is bad

nobody wants perfection—

what do we do when

10-9

stealing our youth and

holding life in nightmare's grip—

monsters are human

10-10

boundaries are set

don't wander too far inland

momma is watching

10-11

seeming linear

chronological order

lifetimes we borrow

10-12

finding our passion

children's laughter and cat's purr...

solace in hard times

10-13

pitch like night in day

harbinger of nightmare dreams

respected not loved

10-14

untold possibilities

dawn with the stream of warm rays

gives morning it's dew

10-15

over-sized hoodie

stretching over tight leggings

giving autumn vibes

10-16

Clowns creep

No escaping

The Funhouse

Smoke and mirrors

10-17

Destined connection

Specially designed

Perfect fit

Limbs intertwined

Puzzling notion

10-18

Pink petals

In Incandescent images

Noticeably nestled near

Kaleidoscope keepsakes

10-19

Gifts given

Without expectation

Are heart-warming

And soul soothing

10-20

Though the frame

b r e a k s

from the f

    a

     l

     l

the memories

remain

10-21

ubiquitous haze–

executive dysfunction

testing my patience

10-22

clear sky, cool morning

lazy stroll along the beach

promise of warm days

10-23

crisp leaves under foot

marshmallow-laced chocolate dreams

autumn memories

10-24

screaming silent sobs

forgetting to breathe until

the pain fades again

10-25

howling with laughter

or keening in agony

lone wolves persevere

10-26

liquid flames

flowing like lava

smooth bourbon

10-27

Three years seems just like

yesterday and thirty more.

How do you feel about that?

Like something just clicked,

like time has no meaning, though

I'd still choose you ev'ryday.

10-28

priorities shift

meld between the two made one

love compromises

10-29

The screams of witches

Bellow through the trees

Weaving spells of death

Hauntingly on the breeze

A warning to all

10-30

arguing across

the penultimate hour's breeze

of love's dying breath

10-31

Dry and neglected

Like crackling hands

On dehydrated souls

November

11-1
Picking up
People
With lines
Of chalk
Easily erased

11-2
time has no meaning
its passage loses value
each minute you're late

11-3

Up all night

dreaming

Lava lakes

between us

Impassable

11-4

she tries newness on

efforts at transformation

escape from past fears

11-5

probably leaves room

for uncertainty and doubt—

thanks, anxiety

11-6

When directions

Aren't direct

They cannot direct

Directionally challenged

11-7

we deal in what ifs

illusions of perspective

knowing is not real

11-8

i wish to forget

the feel of foreboding fate

now not if but when

11-9

ample wordplay to

feed the amygdala's need

writing poetry

11-10

feel how you must on

the whimsy of emotion

you are no mistake

11-11

when two colors blend

remnants of unique hues lost

beware loss of self

11-12

overhanging skin—

battle scars

from life's

fight to

survive

11-13

losing weight carries

the weight of other losses--

yourself and safety

11-14

Gone are longer days

Circadian rhythms

Off kilter dance

evening comes too soon

circadian rhythms off

longer days are gone

11-15

majestic wingspan

flutters in brown, white, and gold

great horned owl takes flight

11-16

Anger rises

Collects like heat

On ceilings

Hurt remains

Close

11-17

Scattered memories

Raked into piles

Like leaves

Pictures of youth

11-18

Hold tight to memories

    Life

        Fades

            Away

Leaving only ruins

11-19

I wrap

Nostalgia

Carefully

Boxed in

A shed

Of memories

———

11-20

I'm a

Flighty

Plastic bag

You're

Steadfast

As a tree

———

11-21

why must simple tasks

be made extra difficult

multi-step hoop jumps

unnecessary stressors

left on the brink of madness

———

11-22

thoughts swirling like wind

hanging on the precipice

push through or let go

———

11-23

Swirled with age

Blanched by the sun's kiss

Life formed rocks

———

11-24

reformation time

shaped in clay molded by hand

silent permission

11-25

novel promises

all the words written today

deadlines looming quick

11-26

boxes and packing

memories stored for later

anxiety peaks

11-27

bake with measurement

each season's recipe calls

add spice with your heart

11-28

Shards intertwining

Unsustainable spinning

Plates on sticks

Beautiful if untenable

My hopes

My dreams

My successes

My failures

A kaleidoscope of fear

11-29

in the public eye

standing behind a table

books fully exposed

11-30

mask long since broken

hormonal upheaval tracks

face speaks emotions

December

12-1
Time winds to a stop
Case of terminal remorse

12-2
Everything
fades away
The moment
The ship
Leaves port

12-3

Sending kisses

like mistletoe thoughts

Crossing infinity's

hopeful wishes

———

12-4

unable to breathe

screaming with lungs full of mud

panic settling in

———

12-5

air freezes

dormant

flowers return

———

12-6

so many projects

writing what comes to my mind

completing nothing

12-7

define it yourself

then revise it as needed:

the plan for success

12-8

freshly fallen snow

silencing my screams in white

dystopian dreams

12-9

wild flames of desire

fanned by untamable winds

spawning dumpster fires

12-10

growing pains come

from vulnerability—

sliced layers of fear

12-11

folding paper cranes

imagination balanced

migration season

12-12

so much to see here

beautiful hues shifting view

where to focus first

12-13

the thin line between

cannot be an opposite

two-sided love/hate

no son opuestos

son niveles varias

Odio y amor

12-14

The threads of our lives

Stuck between

The Fates scissors

And

Mother Nature's

Crochet hooks.

12-15

if given the chance

to start over tomorrow

i'd choose you again

12-16

Let's skip to the good part

You

Me

Forever

12-17

I ride

The tide

Of affection

Like chasing

Illusive reflections

12-18

as I watched his mouth

I bit my bottom lip hard—

thoughts of his kisses

12-19

natural beauty

zest for learning evident

energy boundless

12-20

Your love weaves

Strength into

The threads of

My soul

12-21

get words on paper

creativity flowing

second guess it all

12-22

I caught onto you early

You never let go.

12-23

broken in healing—

uncertainty in the wake

of struggling for air

12-24

Friendships like seasons

shift along changing timelines

some remain favorites

12-25

tiny tornado

leaving happy memories

all over the house

12-26

Surrounded by stillness

My soul screams

In deafening silence

12-27

moist cake, sweet icing

melting along my tongue's length

he feeds my starved soul

12-28

role reversal hurts

parents expect empty nests

kids can't take the loss

12-29

new beginnings don't

require unrealistic resolve

just an open mind

12-30

rumors, gossip, and

illness all have the same rule–

always sip the tea

12-31

Objects in rearview

Incomparable in distance

Heights yet achievable

Bonus Poems

2-29 (Leap Year)

the moment you think
today's nightmare is over
It's today again

Bonus 1 (Roberts Row)

shared delusions hint
motivation unmeasured—
Roberts Row and friends

Bonus 2 (Calling)

Call me a wallflower

as I stand back and watch

Call me shy

because I don't talk in crowds

Call me a bitch

when I ignore your advances

Call me standoffish

for my lack of a smile

Better yet, don't call me...

Send a text instead

Bonus 3 (Frankenstein)

They called her mad.

"Frankenstein," they'd say.

She collected their fears

like jarred specimens

carefully pruned from overgrowth

Preserved in life

To grow like nightmares

beneath the surface

until replanted in the

fertile soil of dreams

Bonus 4 (Summer's Promise)

bright summer promise

oblivious of the storm

confident birds sing

Bonus 5 (Remnants)

Clothes

Heaped on the floor

Remnants of our passion

Bonus 6 (Blackjack)

arguments internal

indecision holding fast

Hit or stay

take a chance

gambling comfort

for possibility

running the numbers

betting the odds

hoping for another

twenty-one

Index of Topics

Not all poems are included in this index, but these are the most common topics. There are numerous poems related to nature, so they are not indexed unless they also relate to other topics.

INDEX OF TOPICS

About the Author

Bobbie Isabel lives in North Carolina surrounded by the people and cats she loves. As a lifelong lover of words, Bobbie is not held to a certain genre. She writes and publishes poetry, fantasy, and children's books that are a combination of the two. She also writes adult romance novels under a separate pen name. When she's not writing, she enjoys spending time with her three-year-old granddaughter, or you can find her in the audience reveling in the language-rich environment of musical theater.

Currently Available Books:

When Can We Be Soft?: Poems of Female Resilience
Lilli and the Nervous Narwhal
Untethered Love
The Maenad—Age of the Forgotten Ones Book 1

Follow Bobbie all over social media:

https://linktr.ee/bisabelwrites

See the website for the latest updates on her writing endeavors and a poetry blog. All of her books are available signed in the shop on the website:
https://bisabelwrites.com/shop

Coming Soon:

Mother's Day 2025: Mother of the Maenad—Age of the Forgotten Ones Prequel Novella

Sometime 2026: Age of the Forgotten Ones Books 2 and 3